the *spirit of poverty*

Freshwater

Freshwater Press
USA

All Scripture references taken from KJV unless otherwise indicated.

The *spirit* of Poverty

Freshwater Press, USA

Dr. Marlene Miles

ISBN: 978-1-960150-11-0

eBook Version

Table of Contents

I pray that this word will be
like jewels for you.

God's Plan

God's plan for us is that we have prosperity, and that abundance is an expected end for us. As we continue to dent our ignorance regarding finances, wealth and prosperity we share in this book, on the *spirit of poverty.*

When this message was originally preached, I had never heard anyone speak on *the spirit of poverty* before, so I praise God for putting it in my spirit and for giving me this to share and to impart to the Body. I understand, now looking at the *spirit of poverty,* why I had never heard anyone teach on it. I've heard people talk *about* it. I've heard people mention it; and you just come to know what it is, because you just know what it isn't.

Whenever we see someone that is not like God, or not like us, or not as we believe or *intend* ourselves to be, we want to minister to them. We want to admonish them to change, or we want to exhort them to good works. We want to share what we know, and even share what we have with them. And so it goes when we believe we see the effects of the *spirit of poverty*.

We often go to the Projects to witness because something inside us knows that Salvation and poverty don't go together. We deduce that an impoverished person must not be saved. We are not always right, but this is either our initial impression, deep prejudice, or both.

So we go to the Projects.

But there are people who have means, affluence and wealth who aren't saved. And there are people who have little, or no means and they *are* saved. Still, there we are in the Projects because poor and Salvation in Christ Jesus don't go together.

We cannot forget that there are saved souls who make vows of poverty, but we are not talking about them in this book. The average person does not want poverty or to live in poverty.

Beloved, I pray above all things that thou mayest be in health and prosper even as your soul prospers. 3 John 1:2

We have been preached the Gospel and by faith we have reached out and received Salvation and Eternal Life through Jesus Christ. Thank God for regenerating our spirits, renewing our hearts and saving our souls. Yet, escaping eternal damnation is only one part of Salvation. The other parts are highly desirable as well: health and relief from poverty. We want health, and we want to prosper, even as our souls prosper.

We have Salvation, and we observe the Great Commission, to reach out to others, offering reconciliation and Salvation through Jesus Christ. It would be prideful of us if we think we are better than the people we are called or led to witness to. It would be hatred if we showed them disdain because of their lifestyle choices or predicaments. Jonah hated

Nineveh and didn't even want to go there to minister to them. Wherever and to whomever you witness you have to be touched with feelings of compassion, else you will not only dishonor and displease God, but you will also get a lot of doors closed in your face.

As we are saved, we are spiritually better off than a lot of people right now, but they can be saved also. No matter when you come into the Kingdom of God – *in* is **in**. Period.

Sequential teaching is critical to proper development. Our church's founding Bishop received Salvation when Salvation was ministered to him. From there, he went on to teach health and faith for healing; that's to his generation. Now, to the next generation, as his son, our Pastor is ministering the next part, which is the prosperity part. So it all goes and flows together. You shouldn't receive just one part of Salvation; receive it all.

Receiving only a part, as precious as any part of it is, especial Salvation, could be why there are so many "religions" today. God told man at certain times, on certain revelations of

God, to build a memorial. They were instructed to build a memorial *to GOD*, because man has a tendency to forget.

It seems a lot of religions spawned from a certain revelation and those who received it built a memorial but never moved forward *from* that revelation. Their revelation may not be wrong, but **God is more than one revelation.** God has more than one revelation. God is progressive and forward moving and will reveal Himself over and again to those who believe Him and seek after Him. God has more than 99 names, each revealing one of His attributes. It would take all of us working together and communicating with one another to know Him in all of His attributes.

Religion is man's attempt to reach God. When God reveals Himself to a people and they build a memorial called a *religion* and never move past it, that memorial is really to *themselves*, not to God. It is a form of idolatry, proclaiming, *Look at us! Look at what and who WE are to GOD! And worse, because we met Him here, or He me us here! They mistakenly believe their man-made religion is **the** only* *way.*

It may be part of the way, or on the way, but JESUS is the only way, the truth and the Life. Man-made religions are never the way to God. Narrow is the path, but it's a path, suggesting progressive *steps*, and forward movement. Not just one stop like God is a quick study. Selah.

When you met your spouse, was one date, one revelation all you wanted from them? Of course not. If we are to be married to the Lamb, don't we need to know Him in *all* of His facets, all His ways, or as many as we can fathom? After all, God is deep. By urging man to move on, even from revelations of GOD, the LORD is attempting to stop man from **worshipping the revelation** but instead to worship GOD.

Many religions are built on one revelation--, just one and the people STOP right there to worship the revelation. Man will worship something, or someone, and now we know, man will also worship *a revelation.* In the world man worships, education, knowledge, and mental prowess. In the

Kingdom we can't worship what we know about God, what He has revealed about Himself; we worship God, Himself.

So revelation is good. It's necessary. But as far as I know God is *still talking*. God is not dead, and never will be; He is Eternal, He is the Only Living God. He is *still* revealing Himself, from glory to glory. Let he who has an ear to hear, hear what the Spirit is saying today. Amen.

Good News of Jesus Christ

So we go to places where we see people who are not walking in prosperity, feeling that we must take them the Good News of Jesus Christ. We may see that they are not walking in the things of God. So in the Lord's great compassion and kindness, He sends us or allows us to go to the Lost.

So we go.

Question: When you see someone who is not **healthy**, does that mean they are not saved? Not necessarily, but without the Spirit of God, we don't know. When we see someone who doesn't have the financial means to take care of what they need to take care of, something in our thinking leads us to believe that they may not be saved. Without the Spirit of God working in us we don't know, but it could be true. There are plenty of folk in church, who are saved, but they don't have *enough*; some may even be in poverty.

We look at the people in the Projects and surmise that they don't have *enough*. As we size up our own condition, we see ourselves as having *enough* or having *access* to enough. We praise God that we have Salvation, we're in the Kingdom, we're in church, we are in a fellowship, and we have **enough**.

Or do we?

In our comforts and good fortune, we want to minister to the less fortunate; we may want to feed them, or clothe them, as the Gospels promote; we want to meet their immediate needs. A hungry man cannot hear you talking, no matter what you are saying. A cold, tired, sleepy man is not very attentive, either.

So immediate needs met; now we tell them about Jesus and Salvation. Well, Glory and Amen.

After that, we should want to *give* them a seed and teach them about prosperity and how their lives can be turned around financially. You want to give them a seed to sow so they can change their lives, they can impact their lives. I've never seen that happen actually. What I've seen is people meeting the immediate physical needs of others, and then bringing them to church, leaving the rest of the needed deliverance and prosperity on that new saint, as if a Baby Christian has any idea how to navigate in those waters. Some seasoned saints don't know how to navigate through deliverance for themselves.

For the sake of instruction, let's say we give them seed to sow--, really God does that, but He does it through *people,* although miracle money is a real thing. But, even though some people sow seed, have you noticed, no matter how much you give them, they still seem not to have? Some of those people are in church, some are not; some may be in your family. It's because of the *spirit of poverty.*

The *spirit of poverty* can be very subtle, sneaky, insidious. It is not easy to teach. Sometimes it is not easy to detect. This demonic *spirit* travels with other *spirits* and can hit a person by surprise. It's like the wind in a way, *not a cold and howling wind that you are fully aware of, but more of a breeze that is almost imperceptible;* you notice the <u>effects</u> that it is causing more than you notice it's presence.

The *spirit of poverty can persist;* even though you may give and give and pour into someone you may be ministering to. They are definitely saved, you watered and watered with the Word of Truth, and you know their heart is right because God gave the increase. However, because of the *spirit of poverty,* they may still be in lack. This spirit causes people to still be without.

Addressing the physical is temporary. The spiritual cause of every negative thing that persists needs to be addressed and dealt with. Many times that takes deliverance. Wouldn't it be nice if at Salvation every single ungodly thing fell off a person and never came back again?

The *spirit of poverty* may be one such *spirit* that persists even after Salvation or it can even come upon an unsuspecting Christian.

Where did this *spirit* come from? Any of several places. It could be ancestral, inherited down your bloodline, by a fore parent's mistake, or knowingly, the ancestor could have entered into an evil contract with an evil person, or entity, for financial or other gain.

An evil person related to you or unrelated to you could have *sent* this *spirit* into your life. Knowing that a curse causeless cannot alight, if the *spirit of poverty* or any other demonic *spirit* stuck to you or your bloodline, then know that there was some evil spiritual glue on you or your family line that drew it and/or caused it to attach to you.

You could have done it. If there is no history of poverty down your bloodline and you are the first one in your family to experience this dearth and lack, then most likely it was you who opened the door for it. I say most likely because curses can have a delayed response, and they can skip generations. It all depends on the curse and how it was enchanted against you, or your people.

There are certain acts in the flesh, certain acts one can do to invite this *spirit*, opening the door for it and also to allow it to stay around. There are also emotions and thought patterns that feed the *spirit of poverty*, tending to the *spirit of poverty*.

We will discuss some of those later, but we are still checking to see if you, or me for that matter, have ***enough***.

Tending To Poverty

There is that which scattereth and yet increaseth and that which withholdeth more than is mete, but it tends to poverty. Proverbs 11:24

Why would anyone ***tend*** to poverty? When we think of the word, *tend*, we think of attending to, listening, hearing, but we think also of cultivating for the purpose of increasing. When a man ***tends*** to poverty, it increases in his life. Unless you know about the *spirit of poverty*, you may be working against yourself causing poverty to increase in your life, instead of decreasing or being dismissed entirely.

We think not having enough to eat, not having a place to live, not having this, that or the other, is poverty; and it is. Poverty *is* not having enough. But not having enough, *what*? Not having enough, *for what*? We will look at that in this book.

We should never look down our noses at others or offend anyone but are we too quick to judge others if they don't *look like* they have enough.

Have you ever thought that there may be people looking at us and saying that <u>we</u> don't have enough?

What is poverty? Poverty *compared to* what? If you have a lifestyle that takes $100,000 a year of disposable income to conduct and you only have $90,000 available each year, you don't have *enough*, but you are not in poverty. You have a certain lifestyle, but your income is not having enough for what you to live as you would like right now. You are in no way in poverty, your needs are surely met, you just don't have enough for your WANTS.

So there is Lack; not having any. There is insufficiency; not having enough. And there is poverty. They are all related, but different. Constantly having lack, not enough for reasonable, basic needs-- is poverty. Constantly having insufficiency may not be lack, it could be bad management.

This book deals with poverty, the not having enough for basic living--, the very basics --a house to live in, food to eat and enough to take care of your health needs, and your family if you have one. Poverty level for the USA for the year 2021 for an individual was anyone who earned around $15,000. per year, or less. For a family of 4 if that family had to live on $33,000. or less, they were considered impoverished. If for none other than financial reasons, it is wise to work, get married, be in a family, live in a family have a certain number of kids, and **DO NOT GET DIVORCED (or separated)**. One family living in two separate houses is pricey and ridiculous. Getting divorced not only is expensive, but it often leaves one or more of the parties *in poverty, it can leave the children in poverty* for obvious reasons. But, also, the *spirit of division,* when breaking a godly covenant, carries with it the *spirit of lack, insufficiency* and *poverty*.

Any action that you can do in the natural that requires MONEY but doesn't bring you money is a vehicle for the *spirit of poverty*.

God hates a broken covenant.

We will discuss other things that tend to poverty later in this book, but first we have to ask and answer if you who are saved, sanctified and set aside---, do you have **enough**?

Do You Have Enough?

God's sitting in the Third Heaven, high and lifted up. As He looks down from Majesty, does He see that **you** have *enough*?

We look at the Scriptures to understand what is *enough*. The Government's standard of poverty is for our flesh man, but we also have to take everything we know spiritually and integrate it together. You just can't listen to one message or read one book and expect that it's going to solve or fix everything.

Do you have *enough*? Are you experiencing lack, insufficiency or poverty? Then you either don't have enough or don't have enough at the right time.

We should have enough because God has promised us ***all things*** that pertain to life and godliness (2Peter 1:3). So now we see there are two categories to evaluate whether we have enough, or not. Do we have sufficiency (enough)? is the first question. Are we suffering lack or are we sufficient in meeting our needs?

Now for the two categories:

- Do we have enough to meet the needs for **<u>life</u>**? *And,*
- Do we have enough to meet the needs for **<u>godliness</u>**?

As proper Christians, now we have to put those things together and ask, again:

- **Do we have enough?**

As humans on our Earth course, we are in a body, so we are concerned with the things that pertain to **life**. We wake up in the morning, look in the mirror, and ask ourselves questions like, *How do we look? Do we have this or that? How do we feel?* Being overly concerned with the natural and all of its flesh, we create in our minds what l will call a big Circle of Life. And as we look in this big Circle of Life and we see (and say) that we need this, this, and this to maintain, Life.

Circle of Life

God cares about that, but we are not just here on Earth for our flesh and our best flesh life. God knows what you need for Godliness and may be wondering a couple of things:

- Why are you **only** asking for money enough to be out of poverty, or even into sufficiency, but not asking for abundance?

- **Why haven't you asked for any Godliness money?**
- Why aren't you asking for the Godliness money **FIRST**?
- Why are you short-sighted, having no Vision?
- Do you not know that you can ask God for Godliness money? or That you need it?
- Or are you just ignoring Godliness altogether because you don't plan to do any Kingdom work while you're here on Earth?

God says He will give you **BOTH,** but you can't just look at what you need for life not giving Godliness a thought. If you don't plan to practice Godliness and budget for it, this could be why *poverty* has come upon you. Disobedience, sin and rebellion all tend to poverty. Ignoring God to celebrate your flesh is idolatry. Poverty also comes in with idolatry.

Yes, I'm saying you can't separate Godliness out of your life if you are one of God's. You are a spirit, living in a body.

(Hebrews, in Egypt would not go to worship without their livestock. They did not take their bodies (flesh) to worship, (serve) God without their offerings, their godliness. *So, if you are saved, how do you plan to live without Godliness?*

Godliness

You may look in the natural at your *nice house, late-model car, designer clothes, thinking, I have all of these things, therefore I am not impoverished.* You are pleased with your Big Circle of Life, the carnal man's natural standard. But God raises the standard. He said He would raise the standard. Just having the things for Life and not having the things for Godliness is not pleasing to God and will diminish your walk, spiritual standing, and anointing, probably sooner than later. Having the things for Life, should only be a little circle—, to God, and it should be to you, as well. But the carnal man makes Life's Circle into a big, gigantic, huge circle.

Note: A saved man can still be carnal.

Here's where it gets really bad. Has God provided **all things** needed for life and Godliness and you've ignored God? That tends to the *spirit of poverty*. That behavior invites poverty. Have you received abundantly from the Lord, but only heaped finances on your own lusts?

No, I'm not saying that you shouldn't have nice things or that you should make a vow of poverty. Actually I believe a vow of poverty is ungodly, based on the Scriptures. Any extreme leading to dysfunction, dissatisfaction, or shame is ungodly. Only the devil would want you broke, busted and disgusted. Jehovah-Jireh, is the Lord Our Provider. El Shaddai is the God of More Than Enough. Nowhere in the Bible have I read that Our God is a *god* of poverty.

Poverty is related to ignorance, sin and

is of the devil. Jesus said, *"The poor you will always have with you."* Listen carefully, if the poor are *with* you, then you are **NOT** the poor--, you are something or supposed to be something *other than poor*, saint of the Most High God. Amen.

Solomon who was very rich did not ask for riches, but he is asked the Lord to give him enough to not have to steal.

Living your flesh **life on your Godliness budget is embezzlement**. If you are paying no tithe, you are living on the Godliness budget. Your hair and nails are done, but there's no tithes, offering, or alms; you are using up the Godliness budget. Godliness comes first. Because of **the poverty of your spirit, your mind, and your soul**—you *say* you love God, but you do not worship Him. We worship God in our obedience, in our giving.

God is looking for those who will worship Him in Spirit and in Truth. Are you worshipping God properly, primarily, foremost, or as an afterthought? Cain brought God an offering that appeared to be an afterthought; in the *process of time,* Cain brought an offering to God. That didn't turn out very well for Cain.

Can't God trust you? If you were an employer how long would an employee last that you can't trust with money, time or anything else? Okay, God is giving us Grace; let's get it together. Solomon said, All the efforts of a man are for his mouth --- but he is never satisfied. If you are diverting (stealing) Godliness money for your flesh life, STOP IT. STOP and repent now.

The things for Godliness should be a much bigger circle than what you need for Life therefore you shouldn't have to divert funds for your flesh life.

Money spent on flesh is temporal, fleeting, here today, gone tomorrow. Money used for Godliness and Kingdom efforts are Eternal. Not only that, money, once consecrated to the Kingdom cannot be STOLEN by the enemy. Without consecrating your money, it's like taking a fat wallet out of your pocket or purse in the hood, at night making it so much easier to be robbed. If you put your money in God's hands, no matter where you are, the enemy cannot access it.

Back to the circles: The Godliness circle/wallet should be much bigger, but by help of the world, infomercials, ad campaigns, and keeping up with the Jones', we've turned it around, thinking we need A LOT to live on, for our best life, our vacations, cars, our children's designer sneakers, and we need all of this—, and then we can just come into the House of God and just be Godly on a shoestring. We think we can just be Godly on a teeny tiny budget.

God is only asking for 10%, but that shouldn't make your mind think, *I can just do a little bit. I can just do my Godly thing over here for just a small amount of money, and I can take all of this 90%—, I need this for **life***.

Although you get to keep 90%, heaping money on your own lusts that should go to Godly projects and endeavors is **idolatry**. The Lord is high and lifted up, not we ourselves.

Circles... Going 'Round in Circles

We must get those circles in focus. Which one's bigger, which one's littler, and you need to understand **that it is more important to do the things that are Godly**. It is more important to do the things that will last. While you are in this body, on Earth, it is more important for you to function in Godliness because you've got all of Eternity to consider. Your choices will determine where and how you will spend Eternity.

God won't look at you and say, *Oh, you lived so good, you had such a nice house, and you really worked the money system. You got paid!* God does take pleasure in the prosperity of His servants, but He's more likely to ask you, **What did you do for the Kingdom?**

God is high and lifted up and He is in

Majesty; it takes a lot of money to operate Majesty. It takes a lot of money to operate the Kingdom of God. It takes a lot of money to get the Word out; it takes a lot of finances, it takes a lot—, a big budget, especially since there are so many entities and forces opposing dissemination of the Word of God. It takes a big budget, a much bigger budget than it takes for *life*.

Your life is important; you are very important to God. Remember, financing Life is easy, compared to Kingdom work. And if it is comparatively so much easier, then we shouldn't have to focus on it so much to make simple things happen.

Jesus was very rich in Heaven, but then He became *poor* for our sakes. He became poor because **all of the wealth down here is poor compared to what's up There**. He gave up so much to come down here for such a comparative little. We know it doesn't take much to live down here, else Jesus wouldn't have called earthly means *poor*. He wouldn't have called it *less* or poor.

Just for fun, Psyche 16 is an asteroid

between the orbits of Mars and Jupiter that is made of solid metal, including gold, platinum, iron and nickel – all the stuff we covet here on Earth. It is estimated that Psyche's various metals are worth $10,000 quadrillion, enough to make each inhabitant of Earth worth 100 billion dollars. There's no shortage of money or wealth in the Universe and God's in charge of IT ALL.

It takes much to operate the Kingdom of God. The logistics of God sending people (you,me) here on assignment may seem complicated, but the Holy Spirit will tell you everything you need to know. God gives people here on Earth, a Vision. He gives you a dream in your heart, He puts purpose in your spirit. God is not cheap. God doesn't give cheap Visions. God doesn't give low-budget versions of the real Vision. God doesn't give marked-down Vision or a marked down *version* of a Vision. He doesn't give, just do this, just a little bit and that will be enough visions. No! God gives the real deal, the whole enchilada. He gives you the whole picture once He sees that He can **trust** you with it. Once God sees He can trust you with a little, He gives you the true riches—spiritually and financially.

Having Enough

It is not until you start looking at your **purpose** that God has called you to, the things that God has put in your heart to do, and the ministries you want to support, that you realize if you have **enough** resources (money), or not. It's not until you look at the works that you're called to do, it's not until you get what you've received in your spirit, into your conscious mind that this work can begin. Ask yourself, What is the work that I am called to do? When you ask that, you will realize that you need a real budget--, a Godliness Budget. Now that you know what you're supposed to do, you will realize if you're in *poverty* or not. And if you habitually don't have enough, the *spirit of poverty* may be at work in your life.

And then, just as we've been looking at

the people in the Projects, going to them, thinking they don't have enough just because they don't live in the kind of house we live in, or drive a kind of car that we drive. We must consider our own *poverty*. The Church at Sardis had **unfinished works**. If you don't have financing for your Kingdom work here on Earth, how will you finish it?

…for I have found your deeds unfinished in the sight of my God. Revelations 3:2b

The letter to the Church at Laodicea in the Revelations read: ***"You say, 'I am rich; I have acquired wealth and do not need a thing.' But you do not realize that you are wretched, pitiful, poor, blind and naked,*** (Rev 3:17)

Have we the nerve to judge others by ***our*** carnal standards and purpose to either make sure they have *carnal* sufficiency so they can "appear" to have "enough" as we do? This can't be God's intent.

Or are we really wise enough to minister to their physical needs knowing that we must supersede that to reach and teach about

Godliness, because we are living it, teaching each man to know his purpose and calling in Christ, once he is saved and to strive for the goals of Godliness?

How do we know the little, old lady who *appears* to have little isn't a supporter of righteous ministries by her tithes and offerings and alms because she's got the spiritual things of God right? And in so doing God supplies every one of her needs according to His riches in Glory. How do we know that she may not care about the outward and carnal trappings of this life, but does have ***all sufficiency***? She has a home to live in that she is satisfied with. She has food and clothing and does not feel stress or worry from not having *enough*. She even walks in good health, which is a NEED provided for by God. She may not live in the Projects, maybe she's Projects-adjacent. Without the Spirit of God, or unless she tells us, we may never know.

We must never walk by sight, but by the Spirit, acknowledging God in all things. This means for us and for others who we may *think* are less fortunate. If the little, old lady is conducting her Godliness as God intends, she's better off than many carnal Christians, she may be better off than most in the Church.

The Projects

Just as we are looking at the people we deem less fortunate or unfortunate, God is looking down at us and saying, **I cast this Vision, this Vision and this Vision—, but they've diminished My Vision to a project!!!** He's looking at us as though _we're_ in the Projects!

We must understand that there is so much more to do.

God has called you, me, us to works. And you need to put your mind on how you will finance your Godliness.

How will you _finance_ your Godliness?

It's not until you look at your vision and your purpose to see what works you have to do, and still have to do. If you don't think you have anything to do, or you think you've done everything already—— you may be sorely surprised in the end.

Everything in, for and from the Kingdom is not free.

Silver and gold have I none, (Acts 3:6).

I think the preacher may have over-simplified this for us. Salvation is a free gift – yeah, but that free gift cost Jesus **everything**.

We get saved on credit, but now that we're in the Kingdom, we've got work to do. So you really do need a Godliness budget.

There you are in your nice, comfy life and creature comforts; you feel like you've got it made. So you throw a $10 or $20 in the offering basket from time to time. Wrong! That's the *spirit of poverty*. Your kids are watching; don't teach them that God is only an afterthought.

If God has not called you to your own ministry and I don't mean to start a church, necessarily, then be a **support** to a ministry that is already launched. Perhaps God has called you to BE a support and maybe only that.

The *spirit of poverty* is a strategy of war, and it's a trick of the devil. Once he gets your flesh **<u>comfortable</u>**, he's got you thinking, you have it made. That is a great deception that can lull you into unproductivity.

Woe to those that are at ease in Zion.

Or you may be blocked entirely from Kingdom work and/or support because of not having enough resources and money. The devil doesn't just try to block your finances, he will also try to block the people that should come into your life to assist you in reaching destiny. Where are your destiny helpers? If some of those "helpers" are supposed to be your staff members and you don't have any money to pay them --, what a horrible cascade of events here, all because of the lack of funds.

This is not at all what God intended.

Money is the lowest power in the Earth, couldn't wc at least conquer that by following the rules that God has established for money?

Recommended: **Power Money** https://a.co/d/12JLCYK and **The Fold** series by this author. https://a.co/d/hsYSus7

Godliness First

It's not until you take that Circle of Life and juxtapose it with the Circle of Godliness that you realize that somewhere in there those two circles intersect, *at least*. Life and Godliness work together, after all, we are spirit navigating this life in a flesh body.

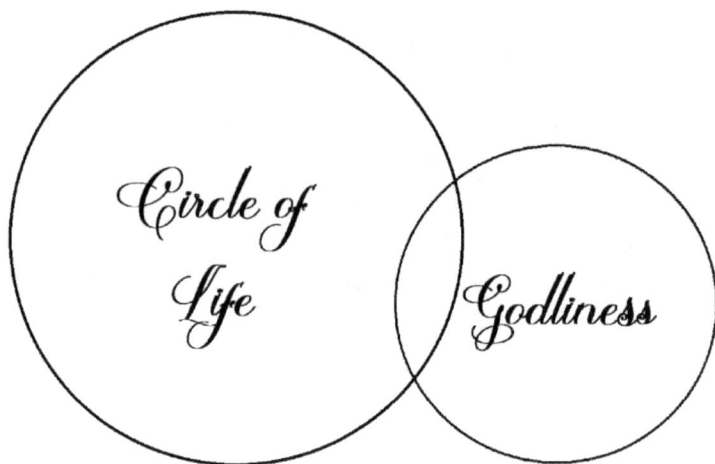

Circle of
Life

Godliness

When you're working Godliness, God will allow you to live in the overflow. In that overflow, you will be able to live abundantly over what you ever thought. Live without robbing God or stealing from the mouths of those to whom He sends you to minister.

Godliness

*Circle of
Life*

Once you put those two Circles together in the right perspective, you then realize that Life and Godliness go right together. When you realize that, that's when you start walking in your purpose. That's when you know that it is much wiser to finance Godliness because what you need for life will come to you, rather than to finance life, because *life will never give you Godliness.*

When I first started working in dentistry, I used to weigh out, *Do I want a big office, or do I want a big house?* Then I realized, hey! it didn't take but a minute! If I had the big office, I could *have* the big house. But if I just have the big house, how am I going to finance the office? So one thing will finance the other, but not vice versa.

Your calling, ministry, vision, purpose, reason for coming to Earth is your **office**. Your lifestyle image is your house. Can your big house finance your Godliness? No, but your OFFICE can finance your physical life.

Unless you're corrupt and have made devil deals, Godliness probably *is* financing your big house in the natural. Godliness is very profitable—, it will also finance your hopes and dreams. We have to get this in our conscious mind. God will give you everything you need, and **more** when you realize that **the Godliness Circle is not the little circle.** It is not the least important, it is not the cheap one.

When you come to realize that all of your life is caught up in and is a result of your conducting yourself in a Godly way, as well as

building the Kingdom, then you'll please God
and all things that you need will be provided
for you.

The *spirit* of Poverty

Some people that you minister to seem to always be in poverty, no matter what. It's because of sin, sometimes; blatant sin, household sin, ancestral sin…. **somebody** sinned. Poverty is under the Curse of the Law; no curse can alight without a cause (sin).

The *spirit of poverty* is like a little flea, it hops on just about every other bad *spirit* or bad sinful act that it can. It's like being a drunk, or being a bar hopper, where you just stay drunk all the time. Then one day you decide, *I'm going to sober up. I'm going to get saved, get delivered and give my life to the Lord.* So you do. Amen, Praise the Lord.

You got delivered from that drunkenness from alcohol, but it's as though the smoke from the bars that you've been sitting in is still on you. It's so subtle because it's been on *you* all the time. *You* can't smell it. And there you are wondering, *I'm saved, I know I got saved, I came into the Kingdom, I don't drink anymore—, I don't **want** to drink anymore. I'm paying my tithes and I'm giving offerings; I'm doing this and this, but it doesn't seem that I'm prospering.* It's the *spirit of poverty*—, it's still **on** you.

That's one of the other reasons you need one-another ministry because somebody will be glad to tell you, that you smell like smoke, if you will receive it. It you are teachable, someone will gladly tell you, if you receive it.

But that's another thing about the *spirit of poverty*, it's got a reason for everything! Oh! The *spirit of poverty* has an excuse or a rationale for everything. You try to tell someone about the *spirit of poverty*—, that's why I started out, *Please don't be offended—*. You try to talk about the *spirit of poverty* and in your mind some of you are thinking, *I'm going to keep on doing it the way I've been doing it because... Grandma did it this way, Momma, Daddy did it this way.*

Did it work for them? Did they leave you an inheritance? Did they bring you up to the starting place where they left off, or did you have to go all the way back to where **they** started and start again from *their* beginning?

The *spirit of poverty* gets embedded in a family, in a bloodline and it affects even how they think. This *spirit* will have a parent tell their kid, *I'm not giving you anything, I had to get everything for myself when I was young and now you do the same. It will do you good.*

Your parents may be loaded, but they won't help you even starting out in life like God is going to pat them on the back for not helping you.

That mindset of not helping you appropriately reflects the *spirit of poverty*. The Good Book says that a good man leaves an inheritance to his children and his *children's* children. The Book doesn't say that the man has to die first.

Let's say he holds on to every penny until his deathbed because he grew up poor and never wants to be poor again. If that man, who outlived his wife, lives to 100 years old and he leaves business start up money to his son who is now 80 --, really? His 80-year-old son never got married because he couldn't afford to. He never had a wife or children, he never moved out of his father's house and got his own, because he couldn't afford to. Once Pops kicks the bucket, his son, Old Junior will be also old, and all alone, because the *spirit of poverty* wouldn't let the old man help his only child. Old Junior will find out that his dad was worth $3 million, and neither of them got to enjoy it, and Old Junior never did the work that he was sent here to do, because of the lack of finances.

Not only that, giving your children startup money and helping them not make the same mistakes you made is love, and it shows Wisdom. Don't let the *spirit of poverty* make you stupid and keep your children and your generations poor.

Ignorance

Poverty and shame shall be to him that refuses instruction. But he that regards reproof shall be honored. Proverbs 13:18

In order to change the *spirit of poverty*, you've got to change your **mind.** You've got to be taught something and you've got to be teachable. The *spirit of poverty* is perpetuated by not heeding instruction, by not being teachable--, by ignorance. Because someone else did it this way, *I'm going to keep on doing it this way.* NO!

Wisdom and prosperity go together. When you know something, you can do something, you can go someplace, you can make things happen, and you can find out what you need to find out for your life and your prosperity.

Prosperity and Wisdom go together. Wisdom will show you how to get rid of the *spirit of poverty* in your life. Wisdom will show you how to be successful in life and Wisdom will ensure that you have good stewardship over what you have. Wisdom will also keep the enemy at bay from attacking your finances. Wisdom will keep you out of sin (Proverbs 3). Sin brings on the *spirit of poverty*.

Laziness

Love not sleep, lest thou come to poverty;
open thine eyes, and thou shalt be satisfied
with bread, Proverbs 20:13

The *slothful spirit* is a *spirit* that will
suffer in poverty. You need to get up and get
out of the house. You can't just hang around
the house and wait for *when-you-feel-like-it*.
You've got to compare faith and feel like it,
because you're never really going to feel like
it. Sometimes our flesh doesn't feel like much
of anything. The sofa is so comfortable…, as a
matter of fact for the past 10 days, I've been
fasting the sofa because it is just so
comfortable.

Ignorance, being unteachable and

laziness all tend to poverty. They all cultivate poverty; they all keep poverty happening in your life.

Another sign of laziness is not taking care of your own stuff. Then we translate that into taking care of other people's things. The Scriptures says, *if you take care of that which is another man's then God will be faithful to give you your own.* That means at your job, at your church, in your community, anywhere you get a chance, God has set that up as an opportunity to bless you. Find something to do, set your hands to do something, even if it's someone else's and God will find a way to bless you. It's as we mentioned earlier in this book—being a blessing to another's ministry so God can in turn bless you and give you your own, if that is what He has called you to do.

Listen closely: People of Color have an extra, extra blessing, and if you could grab a hold to this, I think, you might just shout —. We have, like the Hebrews were in Egypt, **Black people in the United States of America have been taking care of other people's stuff for how many hundred years?**

God has set us all up to be blessed! Do you understand? If you've been taking care of the other man's stuff like you're supposed to have been, you're now set up for a blessing. I am not telling anybody to embrace slavery, I'm not telling anybody to be happy because grandma—, grandpa—, whatever. But since we went through it—, since we had to go through it, since God put us here and left us here for 250 years of slavery, and then since then Jim Crow, in unwarranted servitude. We've been taking care of other people's stuff, now is the time to bring it into your conscious mind, then bring it to the Lord in prayer:

God, I've been taking care of other people's stuff, my daddy been taking care of other people's stuff, my granddaddy been taking care of other people's stuff. My great granddaddy—, You said in Your Word…

Saints: it's all now part of your inheritance!

So, do you have your inheritance? If you bring it to God's remembrance, He can work with it. He can do something for you. If you're in order and you bring it to His remembrance, He can do something for you, because we, of color, as bad as it's been, have been set up to be blessed!

Have you asked God for it?

Have you met the conditions of being blessed by God? You can't just be living some kind of raggedy lifestyle.

Have you prayed it *through*?

Drunkenness

For the drunkard and the glutton shall come
to poverty, and drunkenness shall clothe a
man with rags. Proverbs 23:21

We all know that the party lifestyle and money don't travel well together, even though, in the world that's what they advertise. That's what they have in magazines, TV, movies, music videos and all over the Internet, that if you have money, you can do this, and you can do that, et cetera.

They don't go together. It's a lie, People. I suppose all the saints of God know that. But it's a lie, they don't go together, it's more propaganda from the devil. You may think once you get this amount of money or that amount of money you won't have to do anything else—, ever again, you can just party and relax. The Scripture says it comes to poverty.

Proverbs 21:20 says, *a fool and his money are soon parted*. Well, Dr. Marlene says **that** *a fool and his money, <u>will soon party</u>*.

Most rebellious acts against God do have the *poverty spirit* attached to it, clinging to it. It's subtle but devastating. The *spirit of poverty* is a mindset that sometimes causes a lack of discipline, but sometimes it affects the emotions. It's the way that you are, the way that you've been, and the way that's been transferred to you down your generations. Often transference is how the *spirit of poverty* comes. It's not just something that you did that caused it, it could be generational.

Winds of Doctrine

He that tilleth his land shall have plenty of
bread that he that followeth after vain persons
shall have poverty enough. Proverbs 28:19

Following after vain persons, being led
by winds of doctrine. Doing whatever the next
thing is that comes down the pike that looks
good, is following winds of doctrine. You
decide, *I want that, I want to do that--, i*t tends
to poverty. It leads a person into poverty,
because what someone else is doing that's
prospering them, may not be the thing that God
put in you to prosper you.

Seek wise counsel—, especially that of
the Holy Spirit, and Godly people. Seek wise
counsel and you'll know in your spirit and in
your knower if this the thing that you're

supposed to be doing. Don't run after everything you see on TV or online. You can see one infomercial after the other, after the other, and they promise to make everybody rich.

Do you think the average person is going to point and loudly yell, *"There is gold in them thar hills?"* No, they are going to covet and keep it for themselves.

If their ideas were going to make everybody rich, other people would have thought of it already? Are we to think that these unsaved folk are the only people accessing *Divine Wisdom* for prosperity? I don't think so! If it's the thing for them, then fine. But what God has for you is not only for you—, He will reveal it to you, assuredly. You don't have to guess about it. So this is something else that tends to poverty, perpetuating poverty in your life.

I Wanna Be Rich

He that hastens to be rich, has an evil eye and
considers not that poverty will come upon
him. Proverbs 28:22

Get rich quick schemes, lotteries,
sweepstakes invite and also feed the *spirit of
poverty*. That's why people who win the
lottery don't have any money just a short time
afterward. A few short months later, they don't
have any money, because the *spirit of poverty*
is right there to devour it.

Asmodeus is a ruler *god* over *lust*. The
lust for money, for example. He is over
lotteries, sweepstakes, raffles and the like.
When you participate it is as though he gathers
your name and location in the spirit, and you
open the door for him to come and work

against prosperity in your life. He is wicked, ruthless and takes, takes, takes, steals and leads victims into poverty.

Poverty in the natural is most assuredly *poverty of godliness, confirming that Salvation and poverty do not go together.* In Salvation, the blessings of the LORD should be coming to overtake you. Blessed coming in and going out. Blessed in the city and in the country. In all your ways, blessed.

Other People's Money

Stealing, cheating and messing over other people's money is another way to open the door for the *spirit of poverty.*

The Curse of Poverty

Everything that God says brings on the Curse of the Law, automatically brings on the *spirit of poverty* into a person's life. The Curse of Poverty that has been loosed in a life because of sin.

What sin? Yours or an ancestors; doesn't matter. There are strongholds in bloodlines that need to be broken. There are familial altars emanating curses into a bloodline, some include the *spirit of poverty.* There is evil dedication where an ancestor could have covenanted with evil hundreds of years ago and not even realized that he dedicated his future generations to the devil. There are strongmen and evil *spirits*, such as *python* which brings on poverty big time.

There are spells and curses from

witches, wizards, even blind witches, people speaking evil things into or over your life not even realizing that they are *blind witches*. There are just plain haters who are serious about or dabble in witchcraft who send spells to you because they hate you. They could just be sending spells to Christians to see what will stick and who it will stick to. Whatever the devil sends, know that it is either to steal, kill, destroy, a combination of that, or all of that.

Poverty may be your friend in that it may alert you that something in your life is jacked up and you need to search it out and start praying immediately.

Also in the way of curses, evil human agents may try to curse someone's hands, feet, cage their education, profession, career, destiny, star and or money. They may use padlocks, they may capture, exchange or bury a star.

You don't believe in witchcraft? I don't believe in it to serve in it, as I serve GOD, but I have sense enough to acknowledge that it exists. It is not more powerful than God, but when left unopposed, it is very powerful.

Don't play.

Or, are you just saying because you don't believe in witchcraft that it can't do anything to you? Nope, not true. Are you just saying that because you don't want to pray?

You'd better pray.

There are approximately 1 million people practicing witchcraft in the USA, alone – some of them are your relatives. Some of them look like regular housewives and college kids. Why would a million people believe in something to the point of *practicing* it, if it **doesn't exist?** Thinking in terms of social media, witchcraft has a million followers, and you've got five. You'd better pray, and stay prayed up.

How many more believe witchcraft is real because something has happened to them or someone in their family line? Why is it all though the Bible? Why are you holding out? If you've got a big fat *spirit* of anti-Christ sitting on the throne of your heart, you won't want to pray to God. And you are just that much closer to, more at risk of being used by the devil— becoming an evil human agent yourself.

I thought both the microwave and rap music would be fads. Did my belief make either a fad? Nope.

Is it just that you don't want to pray?

Is it that something has taken your prayer life down to zero?

Yes, I'm saying that poverty in your life or anyone's life could be programmed or cast by evil spells. To understand witchcraft you need to remember your dreams (and visions) and pray to know the correct interpretation of them. God will not leave you flailing, He will tell you what's up and how to handle it, but it takes action on your part.

God is in Heaven; we are on Earth. God has given us everything we need to survive and be victorious in this life. God has given us authority in the Earth. WE have authority, HUMANS. Maybe that's the problem, people think that we are sharing authority with God for Earth. WE have to do certain things ourselves; God is not going to do things that we are supposed to do for ourselves.

If you were away at college and someone came in and messed up your dorm room, do you think your parents will drive 5 or 8 hours to come and clean your room for you? You know your room is a mess; clean it up. YOURSELF!

We wrestle not against flesh and blood, but against spiritual wickedness in high places.

Can We Get There from Here?

Until you learn to *live* **prosperously**, you can't be **prosperous**. You've got to change your whole mindset on *Who am I? What am I here for? How am I going to live?* --, that Godliness thing. People who tend to the *spirit of poverty* are consumed with the poverty mentality, most often lorded over by the flesh. That's where the money goes. They get a windfall of cash, and buy five Cadillacs, a Mercedes Benz and four houses with the lottery money, because they are **tending to their flesh**. Soon, they don't have anything, just that quick. They don't know where it went.

It's spiritual. Those promised, huge windfalls are counterfeit offers— too good to be true, but they are ruled over by little g *gods* that demand sacrifice to them and have full access to snatch all that money back almost at will.

What do I mean by they demand sacrifice and worship? You will spend the money and you will spend it on flesh and foolishness, lose it, or give it all away. Many times bad things will befall the family line, people suddenly die, and et cetera. The demon is demanding sacrifice. You're living it up and maybe without knowing it you are throwing someone that you allegedly love under the bus. That's the sacrifice. Because you love them, the evil, idol *god* chooses this person for you to lose because they want sacrifice and they are empowered with suffering, yours and that of the person sacrificed.

It is a very rare soul who gets that kind of windfall, suddenly, without GOD, **and actually keeps it**. So even if you win a billion dollars today it may be short-lived. Worse, you may be short lived because it is an unspoken "deal" with evil. Once the person who made that deal leaves Earth, their children or heirs will soon lose everything for arguing, bickering and fighting over it. Much less, have they learned how to manage money. Do you remember the old man and the sea? The fish granted him three wishes. Yeah, they weren't lying — these lotteries and windfalls are governed by the marine kingdom.

As long as you're tending to the Circle of Life, which caters to your flesh; as long as you're making that Circle of Life bigger and bigger and bigger, it will tend to poverty.

That doesn't mean don't deny yourself things— Don't deny yourself food unless you are on a deliberate fast. It doesn't mean to suffer unnecessarily. I'm trying to keep this balanced --, not to one extreme or the other. As long as you make that Circle of Life so important, and your main or whole focus, it tends to *poverty*.

Evil Foundation

Then there's the guy who told me that he's a realist who takes responsibility for his own outcomes in life. Because of this, he basically told me he doesn't believe in an evil foundation and that there are no other forces in, around or about his life that affect him in any way. He believes he is either impervious to outside forces, or that they are none. He believes he is master of his own destiny and there are no interferences and no possibility of any. He does not believe in a spirit realm (or realms).

I had been praying asynchronously for him while he was overseas, at his request, but he called me one day expressly to ask me to **stop** praying for him. Which I did. This man's foundation was what made me start looking at foundations – especially my own.

His was clearly one of witchcraft, Freemasons, fraternity blood oaths, multiple divorces, one marriage to a confirmed bisexual witch, estranged family members, estranged children, sexual perversions, money woes. He didn't believe in God, the angry anti-Christ sitting on the throne of his heart would often yell that anyone who believed in God was deceived. But he was beyond frustrated as to why his life wasn't working out as he thought it should.

His household décor was what he probably thought was mancave chic, to me it was more cave man than man cave. Anyhoo, there were evil looking African masks on many walls, swords, dream catchers, owls, pictures of celebrities, framed and hung as if he knew them personally, statues of Pan and whatever gods or goddesses hidden in obscure places, and an entire shrine to a recently lost relative. He was defensive about his décor as if someone had previously called him out on it, especially the ritualistic African goat mask.

Evil foundation.

Oh, I almost forgot, he also had a *spirit spouse* (at least one, but I really think three of them) that confronted me.

We cannot pray against a person's will; that's witchcraft. But, his evil foundation made me look at my own ancestral foundation very soberly. Lesson: Don't be so quick to judge others. Sometimes the life of another person that you may pity, or think is so horrible is a little video of exactly what your life is, but you hadn't seen it until now.

First of all, why was I interested in talking to him? Looking into my own background I found a lot of the **same** junk. Yes, junk. Spiritual junk in my background. What were *my* ancestors doing? Apparently, anything they wanted to. And why didn't I know the spiritual history of my family? Because that's the kind of stuff they keep a secret. Then later in life, when life should be working out for you --, you find out why it isn't by a deep spiritual dive into history, and/or spiritual mapping.

For those who say they don't want to bring a child into the world because of the state of the world, evaluate **<u>yourself</u>**. Evaluate your *spiritual stuff.* It could be that the most unfair thing you do to a child no matter how cute you think they'll be because you both are cute. No matter how smart you think they'll be because you both are smart. No matter how successful you think they'll be because success runs in your families, on both sides, but to bring them into the world of **<u>your</u>** *spiritual junk,* knowingly or unknowingly. What's waiting to ambush that child when they get 20? 30? 40?--, or even 50 years old?

My God! A *spirit spouse* is 85% of the time generational, it travels down the bloodline and has evil **legal right** to have sex with EVERYONE in a family. It spreads mystery diseases and causes people to not only not have decent relationships with real people, but it causes its victims to have to SPEND money. *It tends to poverty.*

To get rid of such requires deliverance, fasting, a lot of warfare prayer and resisting the enemy.

The Promise

This is the third part of Salvation. The *spirit of poverty* will persist if you don't appropriate **all** the parts of the Promise. You have Salvation and health—, you can have prosperity, too. When you receive Salvation, but don't receive the other gifts in the bag then you may still *tend to poverty*. So even though you got delivered from a drug habit, you got delivered from sex sins, you got delivered from something huge, something big, a doozy! Hallelujah! **Why are you still living in poverty?**

You can reach out to Jesus and get saved. You have faith enough to receive, but until your mind knows that there is more to receive, you won't reach out to receive anything else.

If you were in the lowest despairing state of life and you can receive Salvation, be renewed and live, then you also have faith enough to receive full health, then healing for your body and you have faith enough to receive prosperity. As long as you know it's there, as long as you know it's for you. It is for you. You already have the faith for it, you've just got to activate it.

We've got to know that even though all of these sins may come in, sin is a vehicle for the *spirit of poverty*—, any sin. It comes in to block your blessings and eat up the prosperity you may already have.

Quick science lesson: Matter can neither be created nor destroyed. When money flows out of your hand, it doesn't go **nowhere**. Just because it disappeared out of your wallet, or life doesn't mean it *disappeared*. It went somewhere, someone else has it now. If you believe there is a *spirit of poverty,* then you can know that life is spiritual and that there are plenty other *spirits* around. Evil *spirits* are on assignment to steal, kill, and destroy. What do you think they steal? Things of value. Things of value to you and also to them. Time. Peace. Joy. Health. Oh, I don't know--, maybe **MONEY.**

Recommended: **AMONG SOME THIEVES**, by this author. https://a.co/d/6PmiB4h

How can a *spirit* steal **money**? I've done an entire message on my YouTube channel on how the devil steals from you. but there are a number of ways.

(***The*** ***Devil*** ***Loves*** ***Trauma*** https://www.youtube.com/watch?v=pKwFMXXeZQI & ***He Came to Steal*** on DrMiles YouTube Channel.)

The *spirit of poverty* may be trying to take away the stuff you want for life, but MOSTLY it is trying to take away the stuff for Godliness. The devil doesn't care what kind of car you drive, for the most part. He doesn't care about that as much as he's trying to mess with the **Godliness** aspect of your life. You can usually rebound from *life* stuff. People will even help you because they will see that you don't have the things you need in the natural and give you donations, food bank items, clothing. But replacing the things you need for Godliness is another whole thing. If your Godliness is attacked, you may be at great disadvantage.

Godliness:

- Your worship
- Your other Godly disciplines and lifestyle
- Your tithes
- Your offerings
- Your contributions, charity that you give to people.
- Supporting ministries
- Supporting your own ministry (whatever your ministry is— that doesn't mean everybody go preach; it just means whatever your ministry is, because everybody has one.)
- Reading, studying the Bible
- Your Prayer Life

Cutting off supplies, including money is a weapon of warfare. We are in a war. A war broke out in Heaven, and who do you think did that? And then the devil was cast out of Heaven and where did he land? Here on Earth. War is in his nature. So we are still in a war. When it involves money, I call it Financial Warfare.

See these books: **Power Money: Nine Times the Tithe, got money?, Don't Refuse Me, Lord; As My Soul Prospers, Don't Work for Money, The Fold** (series). **Warfare Prayer Against Poverty, Lord, Help My Debt, Don't Orphan Your Seed, Name Your Seed,** and **The Poor Attitudes of Money,** all by this author.

The Devastation

The devastation of the *spirit of poverty* can be substantial. The real devastation will come to your mind when you're at the end of this journey and you realize that you didn't do what you were sent here to do.

Reviewing, the Church at Sardis had unfinished works (Revelations 3:2b). The Church at Laodicea thought they were rich, but they were poor. Do you see how disingenuous or hypocritical it seems to witness to people about what they are supposed to be doing inn the Earth realm, when you as a member of the Church, are not even doing what you are supposed to be doing, yourself?

The devastation of coming to realize at the end of life's journey that you were **poor** all this time. To realize that you were in **poverty**.

Poverty of spirit, poverty of health, poverty of strength, poverty of Grace, poverty of Truth, and/or Peace. Worse, looking down your nose at others who didn't have carnal trappings, but yourself being **poor --, lacking the true riches.**

Sometimes that is the plight of those who get saved on Sunday and believe they are ready for full service in the Kingdom on Monday. We must not be ignorant either of the Word of God or of the devil's devices. The *spirit of poverty* is a slick, strange device that we need to be wary of, wise about and ready to bind up and cast out, in the Name of Jesus.

Godliness is not just coming to church and being here on Earth. You have actions, activities, and you have things to do. Unless you get the prosperity, but not to heap it on your own lusts (the Circle of Life (Flesh)) so you can finance your purpose, what God put you here to do, then you haven't succeeded.

No one can do it for you; they've got to be working on what they were called here to do. Every man is to maintain his own vessel. **Maintain yours.**

The *spirit of poverty*, we are not calling it forth, we are calling it out, so we can tear it down, in the Name of Jesus.

Big Money

Think of God clothed in majesty and sitting on His throne. I think of all the abundance in Heaven, the streets of gold. I think about all of the things of God.

> They saw the God of Israel and there was under His feet, as it were, a paved work of sapphire stone and as it were, the body of heaven in His clearness. Exodus 24:10

Can you imagine having sapphires at your feet? Can you imagine walking on gold? Can you imagine all the majesty of God, the beauty and the splendor? Can you picture all of that? If we've been taught a broke Gospel or that Christians should suffer poverty, we need to change our mindsets. It takes a little while to change a mind. God is magnificent; He's rich. It's incredible. Jesus did not walk around here po'. Jesus and po' don't really mix. Because where Jesus is there is Salvation. Where Jesus is there is health and healing for your body. Where Jesus is there is prosperity. If Jesus is in the place of prosperity, then how can He be poor?

Jesus and prosperity go together. So when your mind gets changed then you understand that Jesus and the Word of God should correspond to wealth, prosperity, the best, and excellence. When you really start to understand that you need to get yourself together in order to finance the Kingdom of God. If you don't have **enough**, how will you build the Kingdom?

If your children go without food, how is that building the Kingdom? It you don't buy groceries for your children, if you don't spend the $100 on groceries for the kids—, $100 is good, but $100—, you know about inflation. $100 does not really finance the Kingdom of God. God is not calling you to suffer, to do without, and be lack so you can take what you were supposed to be using for a reasonable life and try to use it for Godliness.

Godliness

Circle of Life

It's not ever enough. Surely you cannot be thinking that if you starve you can finance your Godliness. The Godliness Circle should be much, much bigger than the Life Circle. He wants you to go out and have more, get more and defeat the *spirit of poverty*, receive the *spirit of prosperity*, the *spirit of wealth* into your own spirit, into your life. He wants you to take the appropriate actions and *receive.*

Just as the wealth of the wicked is stored up (Proverbs 13:22b), it won't be given, necessarily to those people with the *spirit of poverty*, because they will just lose it again.

This teaching is to get you prepared to receive the **wealth of the wicked**. In that wealth are the spoils; the spoils are what you use to build the Kingdom. Put simply, you need **Big Money. But first, you need a big mind to handle big money; you need the Mind of Christ.**

God honors faithfulness, with what He has given you so far. When He gives you a little, He's teaching you to manage Big Money. That's why God tells you to pay tithes and give offerings. He's teaching you to manage Big Money.

I don't know who's got Big Money yet, that's between you and God, but all of us should have it. All of us *can* have it. Big Money—not the gambling kind, though!

Little Money is the training ground. If you can't handle 10% of whatever you make, what are we talking about?

Where Jesus is, there is prosperity, the

spirit of wealth is with Him. He doesn't have the *spirit of poverty,* not Jesus.

If you set out to do what you were put here to do, you get paid. Jesus was doing what He was supposed to be doing and He was getting paid, on top of being who He was, on top of having the *spirit of wealth*, on top of having the Wisemen come and open their treasure to Him when He was a baby. So Jesus was not poor. He may have been meek, He may have been sweet, He may have been blessed, He may have been all of those things, but He wasn't poor.

Jesus was walking around on the Earth as *all this*. Jesus is a Counselor, and an Advocate and a Healer and a Master Teacher. Jesus is Captain of the Host of the Army of the Lord, He's a Consultant to the fisherman. Jesus was all of these things, right here on Earth. Jesus is a Carpenter or a Contractor in the family business, and everybody knows that contractors get paid! Even if Jesus didn't do *anything* in the spiritual, and **we know He did plenty in the spiritual,** He wouldn't have been poor in the natural. If He had gotten paid for even **one** of those jobs.

My point is, are you getting *paid* for your *jobs*? Are you getting paid your ***real*** salary for your real job, your real gifting and talent and skills that God has put in you? That's on you. If you're not, it could be the *spirit of poverty* acting up, making you think, you'd better discount this because people won't want to pay that. **Self-esteem issues tend to poverty.** Although a man not to think more of himself than he ought. Moderation and balance are always the key.

What you have in you is valuable, it is worthwhile. God put it in you. Set your price, name your price, receive your price to the glory of God. Don't mark it down.

God is not marking stuff down. Why would God go through the trouble of making a masterpiece such as yourself and then *discount* you? Set your price. If more people would set their price, then there would be the expectancy, people would realize, *I need this much for real. I can't get by on a shoestring. I need this much to make it in life and to make real Godliness happen while I'm in my real life.*

Set your price, people appreciate you more, if you do. You'll find that the person that you were the nicest to and gave the biggest discount to and did the biggest favor for is the one who will not appreciate it—, they'll be talking about you tomorrow, because most people will not put more value on you, than you put on yourself. Now that is Wisdom for every aspect of your life, business, social, marital and family.

As it pertains to business and career, however, set your price. Maintain your integrity. Walk worthy of who you are. Walk worthy of your calling. Walk worthy.

Idle Talk

In all labor there is profit. But the talk of the
lips is only to penury. Proverbs 14:23

Idle talk tends to poverty. Our mouths
tend more to poverty than almost anything else
we can do after we get saved. Because after
we get saved, we are conscious to walk in
holiness as much as possible, shunning sin,
and trying not to be disobedient. But that
mouth! I know, I've got a mouth.

Do you see that almost every Scripture
has been in Proverbs, that's where the Wisdom
is. Wisdom and prosperity go together.
Wisdom and life go together. Wisdom and
honor go together. They all go together.

Penury is poverty. You could say, talk is

cheap, folk sitting around talking, not getting up and doing any work. What I see there is people who are just talking and talking—, gossip leads to poverty. Because gossip is idle talk.

If you live in a climate that has a cold winter, you will start your car to warm it up before you drive it. You've got it turned on, but it's just idling, it's running, but it's not going anywhere. Idle talk is like that; your mouth is running, but it's not going anywhere. Idle talk. We say things that we shouldn't say, and we say things that we shouldn't mean and that we don't mean, but they may get misconstrued and then they get carried off this way and twisted around that way and turned around and it all leads to and lends itself to the *spirit of poverty*.

We're saying things like, *I wish I had your money.* No I don't. I don't want your money. Do you want mine? No. Because you don't know what I have or what I went through to get it. And my money may not do anything for you as far as what you have to finance. God's put a purpose in you, a Vision in you and

He's also given you the plan on how to do it, if you listen to HIM.

We say idle things such as, *I'm broke.* What's broke? God says you can come to Him, broken. He didn't say anything about "broke." And Jesus even proved it, not a bone on Him was broken—, nothing was *broke* on Jesus.

Things you say that are just catch phrases or slang terms, you want to be clever, cute, mainstream or whatever—, drop that stuff—, it's tending to the *spirit of poverty.* Idle talk, you can think of some more yourself. How about this one? …*'Ain't got this. 'Ain't got that. 'Ain't got* whatever.

If you keep saying you don't have it, you **won't** have it. A man will have whatsoever he says (Mark 11:23). Rather say, *My God supplies all my needs according to His riches in Glory by Christ Jesus.* Someone asks you if you have, don't say you don't have, you may not have the cash in your hands—, **choose your words**.

You don't have to get too picky, but choose your words. *I don't have the cash in my hands right now.*

Don't say you *ain't got* or *you're broke*, especially when it comes to your children, because they will test you. Be brave, be courageous, don't tell you children that you don't have so they won't keep pestering you for money. Instead, tell them, *No, you're not having.* You can tell them in love. *No, that's not appropriate, no, you don't need that, no that's not going to work—, maybe later.* Don't use idle talk and curse yourself to the *spirit of poverty* by repeatedly saying, you *don't have,* you *don't have,* you *don't have.*

By cowardly **lying** to your children about your means, you teach them to tend to the *spirit of poverty* by teaching them that the family is poor or "broke". They grow up believing that this is life. It becomes their expectancy and that is what they will live out. Instead, tell them the truth, *"No, you cannot have $40. for the mall."*

I have. I am an heir to the Promise, aren't you? **I have.** It may not all be manifested right now, but I have. God says

He'll give us all things that pertain to life and Godliness, but He didn't necessarily say He'd give it all to us at one time. So from glory to glory, faith to faith, strength to strength, hopefully not paycheck to paycheck, but we're just moving on in the things of God.

Instead of from paycheck to paycheck, how about from spoils to spoils! Let's go out and win the things of God and earn spoils by defeating the enemy, and one such enemy is the *spirit of poverty*. Once you defeat the *spirit poverty*, you will be amazed at what will just come up to your feet, just to serve you, because you are serving Him. It's going to flow. It's going to be that thing that's been blocked, you know you're supposed to have it—, you don't have it yet.

Some of these mindsets and behaviors have been feeding the *spirit of poverty.*

Back in the older days, in the 40's and 50's they said your *word was your bond*. When you don't keep your word—, when you say you're going to do this and you don't do it, your words become idle. People stop listening to you, you become a joke. Nobody's got time for that hot air. Keep your word and develop the **Fruit of Faithfulness**, develop all the fruit, really. But if you don't develop that then you're just talking—cheap talk. Remember who you are and walk worthy and **talk worthy** of who you are.

Emotions

There are a couple of other things that tend to poverty: Having your emotions out of whack will usually tend to poverty. When you're emotional, your mouth is usually running. You're usually saying what you're going to do to somebody, or you wish you could do. Saying something emotional that doesn't have spirit behind it, will have flesh behind it, and that tends to poverty. It makes you an idle talker.

Idle talker– poverty walker.

Idol Talk

Anything that you put up as an idol will block your view of God. If that happens, I will move, change my position.

Get out of my way!

If you're in my way, between me and God, how will I receive the ministry from God that I need? How will I receive the Word that I need, the encouragement, the love and the peace and all, if somebody's in my way? Anything between me and God is an idol that either inserted itself between me and the Father, or that I put there in ignorance or rebellion.

I can be impressed with Michael Jordan or somebody, but he won't be my idol. And that's not just because I'm a woman, he won't be my idol because he will be blocking my way. He can't do anything for me. Except for one thing. What's that one thing? I'm going to start cheering for all the Big Money athletes. I'm not stating whether Michael Jordan is saved or not, I don't know his status. But all of those folk making all those Big Money incomes, I'm cheering for them—, the wealth of the wicked—. I hope they make a whole lot of money, because when it's time to transfer over, it will be so nice——, I am going to get mine. Let 'em work. He's not my idol, but he can do his job—, the sinner's job is to store up the wealth. I'll cheer them on while they do it.

Again, one of the biggest reasons that the *spirit of poverty* is still here is because people hoard up what they should be giving out. (Proverbs 24)

God is testing you by giving you your salary. Let's say you make 100,000 per year. God is testing you to see if you will give out your $10,000 in tithes and your whatever percentage in offerings. And when you fail that test, the *spirit of poverty* then has place. You're giving place to the *spirit of poverty*.

You are not just giving place to the *spirit of poverty* in **your** life, it goes on and visits to the 3rd and the 4th generations of those who love Him, and to the 10th generations of those who hate Him. You are messing up your children, your grandchildren, your great grandchildren and if they keep doing as you do and thinking as you think, the *spirit of poverty* will be perpetual in your family line. It will never stop. So we look at people who don't give out as they should.

Withholding What Is God's

It's a snare to the man who devours that which is holy. Proverbs 20:25

The Tithe. The tithe. The Tithe.

It says here that it's a snare. A snare is an unsuspecting trap. It's often hidden. It's quick. It's not something that you just casually walk by, and realize that if I keep doing this, it's going to be a trap. No! It's already a snare! Gotcha!

But God is merciful—, you can get out of it. He will rebuke the Devourer for your sake, *and* you can renounce the *spirit of poverty- bind it up, cast it out.*

But that's one of the main reasons, that people hold on to the tithe is the *spirit of poverty.* This *spirit* has a reason for everything. *If I give them this, what am I going to put in my gas tank this week? If I give this, what will I eat for lunch?* The *spirit of poverty* has a reason. That's why the Scripture says, lean not to your own understanding, but acknowledge God. If He's dropping it in your spirit to give this, do this, then that is what you're supposed to be doing.

The Poor You Have with You

In the Gospels there was a woman who had an alabaster box—, *ooh*, I think about that woman a lot, actually. She took that precious ointment in that precious box—, actually that box was precious too. She anointed Jesus' feet with the expensive contents of that box. What if Jesus was coming to your town and it was your day to anoint His feet, or whatever your ministry is that you're supposed to ministry DIRECTLY to Jesus, but you didn't even have an alabaster box with precious ointment in it because you were too po'?

You may be lamenting then, *I sure wished I had saved up and got that box, ooh, I saw it and my first mind said to get it. But then*

I had a reason why I didn't get it. 'Cause my kids had to go to camp—, or whatever.

What if your ministry opportunity comes and you're not prepared because you've been tending to life and not tending to Godliness!

Jesus said right then, **The poor, you will always have with you,** (John 8, Mark 14:3).

That goes back to that mindset teaching. Jesus wasn't poor. If He were poor, that would be the same as me saying, *The Blacks you will always have with you.* Well, I'm Black. Or *the women you will always have with you.* I'm a woman. Jesus wasn't poor; if He were poor, He wouldn't have been talking in that *person.* The poor, you will always have with you. Those people who don't choose to be saved and receive the gifts and promises of Salvation. Those people who don't choose to do the will of God will be poor. Because the *spirit of poverty* is going to help them stay poor.

You have to be **<u>prepared</u>** so when your opportunity, your time of ministry comes, when it's your season, you've got means.

Until your season, perhaps you are to support. Or maybe that *is* your ministry—, to be a support.

I think back to the times when Jesus was here, who would I have been in the times of Jesus? What would I have done? What would have been my ministry? And the beauty of it is, we **are** in the times of Jesus, and we all are who we are and we all have the ministries that we have, so all we have to do, is do it.

I am not saying to shun the poor. You should give to the poor; you should minister reconciliation and salvation to the poor. You should witness to the poor, even in the Projects. You should always do the work of an Evangelist. But, be strong. Have on the full armor of God, especially the helmet of Salvation, the breastplate of Righteousness and the Shield of Faith so you don't adopt their mindsets, instead of teaching them yours. Guard your head and your heart when you go out into the fields of the Lord. And go with Covering.

The *spirit of poverty* makes you ask, Life *or* Godliness. God says you can have

BOTH; Life **and** Godliness and those things that pertain to BOTH. Only the enemy tries to separate the two in order to confuse your mind. And the average human being will choose their flesh.

But we aren't average!

All of these things keep ministering to the *spirit of poverty*. So we have to make sure that we are aware, we get it down in our spirits, that it's second nature, and even if we have to go to our notes that we just wrote down today and look at it again--, for a time. But after a while it should get down in our spirit.

Good Ain't Bad

I would be remiss if I didn't say that especially as the Black race, all the slang terms, all the things we say backwards... the *spirit of poverty*—, it's a trick, good is bad, bad is good, dark is light, whatever! All of that backward stuff, it tends to the *spirit of poverty*. Stop it. Please!

No, I am not saying that is what caused the *spirit of poverty* to come upon the Black race. I don't have to say that— you have read the rest of this book, right? But your confession is crucial to drawing or repelling the *spirit of prosperity*, or the *spirit of poverty*. I've told you before, watch your mouth!

One will put a thousand to flight. God has sent ministering spirits to minister to you—, angels. When you say something, they go out and try to make it happen, even if you say something totally, not the Word of God! We will judge angels, they are not going to judge us. You say something backward--, they will try to make it happen for you. Did you know that? They don't say, *Oh, they must have meant... Or, let me turn that around.* They can't do that, they don't have that authority. They go and try to make whatever you just said happen for you. If you say it enough, if you've got faith enough for it, it will come to pass. And you're wondering why your life is like it is? It's that mouth.

Transference

The *spirit of poverty* is transferred a number of ways:

- Generationally.

If you are walking in the *spirit of poverty,* you can transfer it to your generations, just by them being born of you.

- Association

By them living in your house, under your roof and receiving how you think and how you do things, how you walk and talk, how you handle things, it can be transferred that way.

- Relationships

Who you're hanging out with.

- Marriage

Let's say you got over the biggest sin of all, and to all of us, it should be whatever we were committing at that time that God was so gracious to forgive us of when we received Salvation. And now it's time for you to get married—. People, talk about your pre-nuptials. You need to find out if that other person is suffering under the *spirit of poverty*. You need to do a whole spiritual background check, not to condemn, not to cast aspersion, so you can know how you're going to meld together. Because one of the biggest problems in a family is when you have a husband and a wife, and one wants to tithe and the other one doesn't.

The *spirit of poverty* will lead to a big fight.

As a matter of fact, they say finances is the number one reason why people break up. Talk about your pre-nuptials. You need to find out what's happening in the spiritual life of the other person that is so good looking or so… whatever they are that you just want to spend your whole life with them.

Rich & Famous- Maybe, Maybe Not

You can't take *your* poverty mindset and say, those are poor people over there, I'm going to hang out with rich people, so it can rub off on you. It might. But first you've got to get rid of the *spirit of poverty* so you can receive the *spirit of wealth*. You've got to be teachable. You can't just hang out with the wealthy people, without learning anything. Don't be offended, be teachable.

It's not until we look at ourselves and what we are called to do that we realize if **we** really have enough or not—, whether we are in poverty or not. It's not until we look at how God is living that we realize that our own righteousness is as filthy rags… that we realize that our own wealth is not all it needs to be. It's as though we are living in rags compared to how God lives. And when He calls us to bring forth a Vision on the Earth, and to finance a Godly Vision, that's not necessarily going to be cheap. Churches can minister to people and lift them up, but none of us are supposed to stay in the same place where we come in. We are to step up and be supporters, providers, and suppliers of the provision to bring forth God's ultimate Vision in the Earth--, and that's a really big Circle.

When you do what you're supposed to do related to Godliness, all things that you need will automatically be provided in your little Circle.

Seek first the Kingdom and all of its righteousness and all these things will be added unto you.
Matthew 6:33

Godliness

Circle of Life

Warfare & Deliverance

Review: Repent of robbing God. That is the #1 thing that opens the odor for the *spirit of poverty*. Repent for your ancestors on both sides of your bloodline back to at least 10 generations, all the way back to or before Adam & Eve is best.

Renounce disobedience, pride, idolatry, and other works of the flesh. Bind and pull down stinginess, and cheating.

Loose generosity; walk in it. Resist the devil. Keep the counsel of the Word of God, as well as this book to avoid those things that tend to poverty.

Poverty is not always obvious, it piggybacks on with every other evil *spirit* that it can, pride, hatred, jealousy, et cetera.

Always rely on the Holy Spirit to bring

you under conviction so you can repent quickly, and change.

Dear Reader

Bless you for acquiring and reading this book. I pray that it has opened your understanding.

May you always have enough, sufficiency, more than enough, and abundance to fulfill your life and godliness to the Glory of God.

For more specific prayers to combat the *spirit of poverty*, see **Warfare Prayer Against Poverty** on Warfare Prayer Channel on YouTube.
https://www.youtube.com/watch?v=6pMqbFRXgL4&t=7s
The prayers on this Channel are prayed in first person, so you can pray along and pray against this *spirit* to get it out of your life and your family's life.

If you would like a transcript of this involved warfare prayer, it is available on amazon/Kindle as an eBook or paperback.
https://a.co/d/d6sf3ZC

Christian books by this author

AK: Adventures of the Agape Kid

AMONG SOME THIEVES

As My Soul Prospers

Behave

Churchzilla (The Wanna-Be Bride of Christ)

The Coco-So-So Correct Show

Demons Hate Questions

Devil Weapons: *Anger, Unforgiveness &*

Bitterness

Do Not Orphan Your Seed

Do Not Work for Money

Don't Refuse Me Lord

The FAT Demons

got Money?

Let Me Have a Dollar's Worth

Living for the NOW of God

Lord, Help My Debt

Lose My Location

Made Perfect In Love

The Man Safari *(Really, I'm Just Looking)*

Marriage Ed., *Rules of Engagement & Marriage*

The Motherboard: *Key to Soul Prosperity*

Name Your Seed

Plantation Souls

The Poor Attitudes of Money

Power Money: Nine Times the Tithe

The Power of Wealth

Seasons of Grief

Seasons of War

SOULS in Captivity

Soul Prosperity: Your Health & Your Wealth

The *spirit* of Poverty

The Throne of Grace, *Courtroom Prayers*

Time Is of the Essence

Triangular Powers (4 book series)

Warfare Prayer Against Poverty

When the Devourer is Rebuked

The Wilderness Romance

Notes: